MAKE ART WITH Nature

PIPPA PIXLEY

Senior Editor Carrie Love
Project Art Editor Victoria Palastanga
Editors Abi Luscombe, Clare Lloyd, Abi Maxwell
Designers Sunita Gahir, Holly Price,
Charlotte Jennings, Sif Nørskov, Ann Cannings
Senior Production Editor Nikoleta Parasaki
Senior Production Controller Ena Matagic
Jacket Designer Victoria Palastanga
US Editor Jane Perlmutter
US Senior Editor Shannon Beatty
Managing Editor Penny Smith
Managing Art Editor Diane Peyton-Jones
Deputy Art Director Mabel Chan
Publishing Director Sarah Larter
Publisher Francesca Young

First American Edition, 2024
Published in the United States by DK Publishing,
a division of Penguin Random House LLC
1745 Broadway, 20th Floor, New York, NY 10019

Text copyright © Pippa Pixley 2024
Layout and design copyright © 2024
Dorling Kindersley Limited
24 25 26 27 28 10 9 8 7 6 5 4 3 2 1
001–336475–Mar/2024

Published in Great Britain by Dorling Kindersley Limited

A catalog record for this book
is available from the Library of Congress.
ISBN 978-0-7440-9194-6

DK books are available at special discounts when
purchased in bulk for sales promotions, premiums, fund-
raising, or educational use. For details, contact:
DK Publishing Special Markets, 1745 Broadway,
20th Floor, New York, NY 10019
SpecialSales@dk.com

Printed and bound in China

www.dk.com

CONTENTS

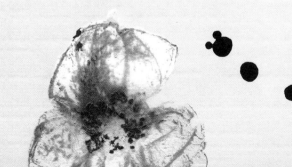

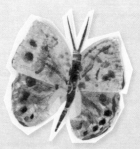

HOW TO BE A NATURAL ARTIST

Raise your hand if you love art.

Raise your other hand if you love nature.

Wonderful—I love those things, too!

HI, I'M PIPPA!

I grew up in the city but I've always loved being outdoors. Are there any wild spaces near you? As a child I discovered a whole world of giant trees and teeny, tiny flowers. I would dig for wiggly worms and listen to the beautiful birdsong, coming home happy and very muddy! The things I saw, heard, and felt found their way into my art.

Now I've grown bigger, but I still have the same sense of wonder when I'm around nature. I go outdoors every day, searching for amazing stuff to draw in my sketchbook or to jot down in my journal. I always find natural treasures—a fallen twig that makes a perfect paintbrush, or a pigment-rich pebble I can paint with. Did you know that you can make your own art materials from natural items? Have you tried reusing things like vegetable peels and old envelopes to make art?

In my life as an artist, author, and photographer I aim to work in a sustainable way, in harmony with our environment. We are the guardians of our wonderful planet and all that lives upon it. Let the wild beauty that you find in nature inspire you to make art, and make a difference. The little choices we make have a BIG impact.

So, try the projects in this book, and discover how to be a natural artist. GO EXPLORE, and HAVE FUN!

Pippa xx

Before you begin

NOTE TO CHILDREN

The projects in this book are fun to create, but make sure you follow the instructions closely. Wear an apron to avoid staining your clothes. Never go anywhere by yourself, always be extra careful when making art with nature, and **ask an adult** to do any of the following:

- Cut materials with sharp scissors.
- Handle any hot liquids.
- Use items that will stain your skin, clothes, or furniture.
- Stick anything down using strong glue.
- Grate fruits or vegetables.
- Use hot objects, such as the stove or an iron.
- Slice anything with a sharp knife.

NOTE TO ADULTS

Children will need supervision when making projects from this book, especially younger ones. You know your child's dexterity and level of skill, and may need to adjust the tools or level of support accordingly. Guide them on how to do the activities.

Always accompany your child when exploring and foraging for items to create art. Follow the rules for where you live. Some places do not allow flowers to be picked. Be aware that it can be illegal to take home some natural materials from a beach, so do the activities while you are there. You must be with your child **at all times** when they're near water, such as at the beach, or by rivers and lakes.

WHEN YOU SEE THIS RED WARNING BOX, BE EXTRA CAREFUL TO FOLLOW THE INSTRUCTIONS IN IT. THE HEALTH AND SAFETY BUNNY APPEARS THROUGHOUT THE BOOK TO GIVE YOU GUIDANCE, TOO.

HELLO!

Useful stuff

Throughout this book we will find tools and create art using natural materials. But before we go outside we also need to collect some key items from around the house that might come in handy!

Cardboard

Tape

Sketchbook

Pencil

plain paper

Card stock

Scissors

Coloring pencils

Scrap paper

PVA glue

Paintbrush

Journal

Glue stick

String

plate

Mixing bowl

paper towels

Measuring spoons

Large bowl

Measuring cups

Coffee filters

Strainer

mortar and pestle

Small bowl

Rolling pin

Wooden spoon

parchment paper

Jars

BE CAREFUL, SOME TOOLS ARE SHARP OR CAN GET HOT, SO ASK AN ADULT TO HELP YOU.

Grater

Saucepan

Sharp knife

Blender

Artists' tools

There is an amazing variety of artists' tools waiting to be discovered or created—you just need to know what to look for.

HOMEMADE BRUSHES

These brushes are made from twisted twine, fronds of seaweed, wiry wool, and fibrous grasses attached to twig handles.

GUM ARABIC MEDIUM

You'll need this recipe for some of the activities in this book.

- 10 tbsp. water or half a jar
- 5 tbsp. gum arabic
- 1 tsp. honey (optional)
- 1 tsp. glycerine (optional)
- 1-2 drops of clove oil (optional)

POINTY STICKS

You can use a pencil sharpener to give an ordinary twig a fine point—perfect for scribbling and writing.

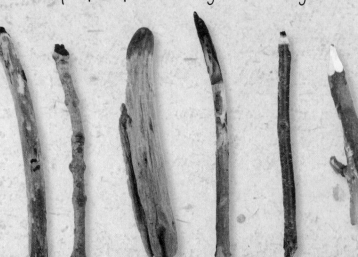

NATURAL TEXTURES

Dried seaweed, seedpods, grasses, and sprigs can all be used for printing and painting. They create interesting textures and add depth to your art.

ASK AN ADULT TO HELP WHEN USING FIRE AND CANS. CANS CAN BE SHARP, SO MAKE SURE AN ADULT COVERS THE EDGES WITH DUCT TAPE.

STONES

Smooth, hard pebbles from a stream or the beach can make an excellent mortar and pestle for grinding pigments. You can also test softer rocks by rubbing them on a harder rock to see what marks and colors they make.

BURNED STICKS

Ask an adult to char the end of a stick, and when it has cooled down you can use it as a charcoal pencil!

CANS AND JARS

Don't throw them away—they are perfect as paintbrush containers or water jars.

NATURAL PAINTPOTS

You can use a shell or an acorn cup as a container for your homemade paint. You can also use any old plate as a mixing palette.

9

All about color

There are so many different colors and shades around us, and we can recreate them for ourselves by mixing paint. This color wheel shows what colors you can make when you mix two different colors together.

Colors that are opposite each other on the wheel are called contrasting, or complementary colors.

Between each primary color is a secondary color, which is made when the two closest primary colors are mixed together.

COLOR WHEEL

Blue

Green

Purple

Yellow

Red

Orange

PRIMARY COLORS

All colors can be made from three colors: red, blue, and yellow. These are called primary colors.

SECONDARY COLORS

Green, purple, and orange are secondary colors. They are made by mixing two primary colors together.

TERTIARY COLORS

Tertiary colors are made when a primary color is mixed with a secondary color. For example, lime is made by mixing yellow and green.

WARM OR COOL

Red, orange, and yellow are warm colors that remind us of the sun or fire. Green, blue, and purple are cool colors that make us think of cold things, such as ice.

TONES AND SHADES

+ white   + black

Adding white makes lighter tones of a color...

...adding black makes darker tones and shades.

Drawing tips

Drawing is easy—just a few lines, squiggles, scribbles, dots, and dashes, can be used to create lots of exciting stuff! Let's begin by wiggling our fingers to warm them up, then we're ready to get started.

Dots

Dashes

Curves

Zigzags

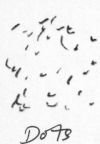

Wiggles

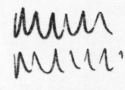

Shading

Scribbling

Crosshatching

Can you find any of the marks above in this hedgehog drawing?

pencil tip

Side of tip

BIG AND SMALL

Experiment by using only your fingertips to make small, controlled pencil marks. Then, make big marks by relaxing your shoulder and moving your whole arm more loosely.

Make dark, bold lines for the beetles' body.

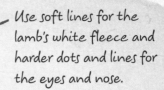

Use soft lines for the lamb's white fleece and harder dots and lines for the eyes and nose.

Try loose upward lines for lift and movement.

Use heavier lines for the bird's claws, and eyes.

PENCIL GRIP

Do you grip the pencil tightly near the tip, like you do when you are writing? Try holding the pencil lightly, in the middle. Then try holding the pencil by its farthest end.

Mouse in nest

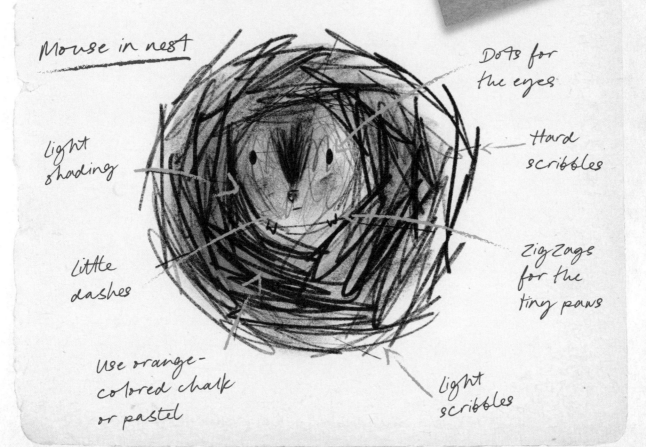

Light shading

Little dashes

Use orange-colored chalk or pastel

Dots for the eyes

Hard scribbles

ZigZags for the tiny paws

light scribbles

Making paint colors

All paint is made with a pigment mixed with a binder. A pigment is the color from the fruit, vegetables, spices, or soil. A binder is the gluey stuff that holds paint pigments together. There's a rainbow of paint colors you can make from fruits, veggies, spices, and even mud. So, grab your apron and get started!

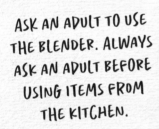

ASK AN ADULT TO USE THE BLENDER. ALWAYS ASK AN ADULT BEFORE USING ITEMS FROM THE KITCHEN.

PINK PAINT

There are so many shades of pink. Follow these steps to make a reddish-pink paint color from a beet.

YOU WILL NEED

- 1 cooked beet
- blender
- bowl
- drop of honey
- pinch of salt
- paintbrush

1 Put your beet into the blender and blend it into a liquid.

2 Pour the mixture into the bowl. Add the honey and salt.

3 Start painting!

Beet

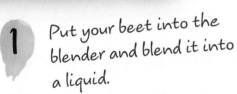

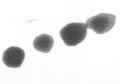

Blackberries

Cherries

PURPLE PAINT

For mauve, lilac, or plum colored paint, switch from your beet to other fruits or vegetables, such as blackberries, blueberries, or cherries.

TIP
Just squash berries with your fingers to see their color. Some berry paint will start off pink and change to purple over time—magic!

Blueberries

BLUE PAINT

It is hard to make blue paint using fruits or vegetables. Instead spirulina can be used to make a range of blue shades.

Spirulina paint

Paint binders

These items are known as binders. We can use them to transform our pigments.

BINDING MEDIUMS
Gum tragacanth and water
Gum arabic and water
Cornstarch and water

WATERCOLOR PAINTS
Gum arabic
Gum tragacanth
Honey
Glycerine
Sugar and water

PRINTING PAINT THICKENERS
Cornstarch
Yogurt
Gum tragacanth
Leaf gelatin

COLOR CHANGERS OR ENHANCERS
Baking soda
Vinegar
Lemon juice
Cream of tartar

GLUES
Rice flour and water
Sticky sushi rice starch and water
Plain flour and water

15

More paint colors

It's easy to mix paint colors from ingredients in your fridge or pantry. Find some green veggies and golden-colored spices, and start blending!

GREEN PAINT

Don't like eating your greens? Turn your leftover veggies into gloriously green paint instead!

1 Place your green vegetable into the blender and puree it.

2 Pour into a bowl. Stir the honey in. You have green paint!

Broccoli

Kale

! ASK AN ADULT TO USE THE BLENDER. ALWAYS ASK AN ADULT BEFORE USING ITEMS FROM THE KITCHEN.

TIP
Blend each veggie separately, then try mixing them together to see what shades you can make.

Mint

Spinach

YELLOW AND ORANGE PAINTS

You can make bright yellow and orange paints from so many spices. What spices will you choose?

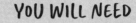
ASK AN ADULT TO HELP WHEN USING WARM WATER. SPICES CAN STAIN YOU, YOUR CLOTHES, AND WORK SURFACES.

YOU WILL NEED

- 1 heaped tbsp. dried spice, such as turmeric
- jar
- 2–3 tbsp. warm water
- couple drops of honey
- spoon
- paper

1 Pour your spice into a jar, add the warm water, and let it sit for 15 minutes.

2 Add the honey, and mix together using a spoon.

3 Brush your paint onto a piece of paper. When it's dry, rub off any residue. Good job, you have made spice paint!

TRY IT OUT! I'M MADE FROM TURMERIC.

Guinea pig

Mix a pinch of saffron with a dash of water for a vibrant yellow paint.

Ask an adult to make pencils from thin pieces of fresh turmeric. Shave off the peel at the end with a spoon.

Saffron

Turmeric root

Brown paint shades

Making brown paint is really simple. Here's how to use a slice of burned toast and some cocoa powder to make different brown tones.

ASK AN ADULT TO BURN THE TOAST AND SCRAPE THE TOAST USING THE BLUNT KNIFE.

BURNED-TOAST BROWN PAINT

Have you ever burned toast? Don't throw it away—you can make paint from the burned crumbs! Let's learn how.

YOU WILL NEED

- blunt wooden knife
- 1 slice of burned toast
- small plate
- few drops of water
- spoon

1 Using your blunt wooden takeout knife, carefully scrape a layer of burned toast crumbs onto a plate.

2 Add water to the crumbs. Using a spoon, mix the water and crumbs together to form a paste. You have paint!

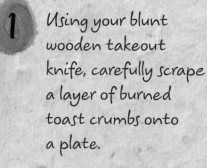

Burned toast paint bear

YOU WILL NEED

- 1 tbsp. cocoa powder
- small bowl
- 5 tsp. water
- spoon

COCOA-POWDER BROWN PAINT

Do you love hot chocolate with whipped cream? Did you know you can also make paint from your cocoa powder? All you have to do is add water.

1 Put the cocoa powder into a bowl.

2 Add the water and mix. Now you have brown paint!

Cocoa powder paint beaver

MORE TO MAKE

Burned toast paint swatches

Mud paint vole

You can also make brown paint from mud. If muddy potatoes get a little wet, just dip your paintbrush in and start painting! Try creating a tiny vole.

Chalky paint

Did you know you can make thicker, chalkier-looking paint using just a few ingredients you probably have hiding in your kitchen? Give it a try!

YOU WILL NEED

- 1 cup cornstarch
- ½ cup water
- mixing bowl
- spoon
- 6-well paint palette
- couple drops of natural food colorings
- paintbrush

1 Combine the cornstarch and water in the bowl. Stir the mixture until it has a smooth, even paintlike consistency.

paint palette

2 Divide the mixture equally between the six wells in your paint palette. These will become your paints.

TIP
You can also use soy milk or cottage cheese to make paint too!

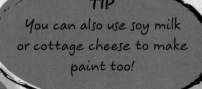

3 Add your different food colorings to each well. Mix the paints to make sure you like with the colors. Now start painting!

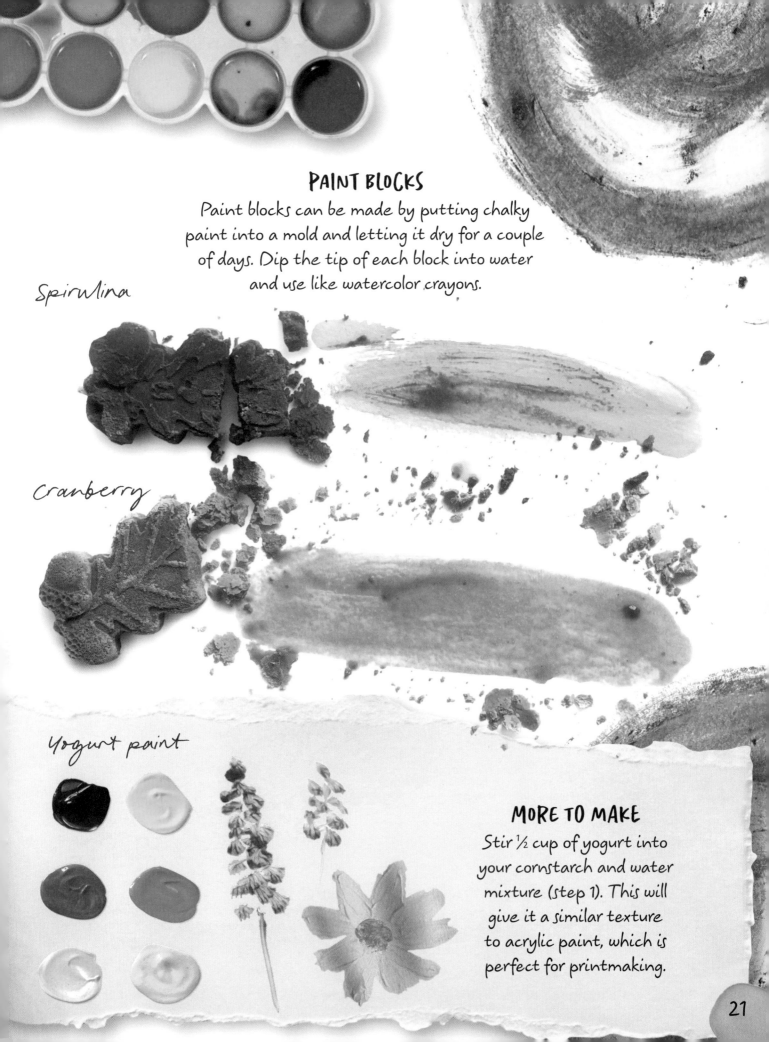

PAINT BLOCKS

Paint blocks can be made by putting chalky paint into a mold and letting it dry for a couple of days. Dip the tip of each block into water and use like watercolor crayons.

Spirulina

Cranberry

Yogurt paint

MORE TO MAKE

Stir ½ cup of yogurt into your cornstarch and water mixture (step 1). This will give it a similar texture to acrylic paint, which is perfect for printmaking.

Journaling

DRAW
Grab your pencil and your journal, and draw anything that excites you.

Song thrush

Wings

Beak

Speckled chest

Claws

Keeping a journal tells a story of where you've been and what you've seen. It's a good idea to always carry your journal and pencil with you, ready to record your outdoor adventures. So let's get started!

YOU WILL NEED

- journal
- scrap paper
- pencil
- tape
- fallen cones
- leaves
- lichens
- petals

What wildlife do you see? What colors inspire you?

COLLECT
Stuff your journal full of treasures that you find: leaves, lichen, and petals. Only take things that have naturally fallen on the ground.

Nettle

Oak leaf

TAPE
Tape is super useful for sticking objects and sketches into your journal.

Alder "cones"

Rose

petals

leaves

Daisy

White petals

Yellow center

LABELS
Label your drawings and the items you collect on your adventure.

NOTES
Jot down little details to remind yourself where you found things, and how they smell or feel.

⚠️ ALWAYS GO OUT WITH AN ADULT TO DO JOURNALING. OBSERVE, BUT DO NOT TOUCH MUSHROOMS.

COLOR TESTS
If you find any natural pigments, test them out in your journal and label them clearly.

Clay

Charcoal

Red oxide

Mushroom

From the kitchen

Did you know that there is an amazing variety of vibrant artists' colors hiding in your own kitchen?

Together, we'll extract rich colors from fruits and vegetables, spices and herbs—coffee-brown, beet-pink, carrot-orange, turmeric-yellow—and we'll use them to create some lovely marks and art. Nothing will go to waste as we discover fresh uses for old vegetable peels and empty egg cartons.

There's a bit of science and magic in the processes of making invisible ink from lemon juice, or in watching your vegetable ink change color from purple to teal to pink as you add different secret ingredients!

So, wash your hands, tie on your apron, and let's get busy…

Kitchen colors

You'll be amazed at the colors and textures you can create from everyday items, such as spices and dried beans. So, take a peek at what's hiding in the back of your kitchen cabinet—delve among the packages and jars to see what you can find.

PAPRIKA
Mixed with a splash of water, this smoky-scented spice makes a beautiful burnt-orange hue.

TURMERIC
When water is added to ground turmeric, it makes a beautiful, rich yellow color paint.

SPIRULINA
This edible marine algae comes in powdered form, and makes an excellent bright-blue or green paint when water is added to it.

CINNAMON AND COFFEE
Mix water with ground cinnamon sticks, cocoa, and coffee to get a rich variety of warm tones, ranging from beige to black.

DRIED BLACK BEANS
Soak a few of these beans in a jar of cold water to make black ink. Adding baking soda (an alkaline) makes a purple ink. Adding lemon juice (an acid) creates a lavender color.

RED
Beet power can be used to make red food coloring.

BLACK
Vegetable carbon is made from charred vegetables, and is used in some black food coloring.

NATURAL FOOD COLORINGS
Do you have a bottle of food coloring? Check out the ingredients list on the label. The color often comes from nature. Mix a drop of food coloring with a little water and you'll have an ink to paint with.

GREEN
Plant-based chlorophyll can be squeezed from kale or spinach to make green coloring.

YELLOW
Curcumin is yellow and can be extracted from turmeric roots.

food coloring

In this book you will explore the science of homemade inks. Add a few special ingredients and watch your ink colors magically change in front of your eyes!

LET'S MAKE SOME INK!

Coffee ink

Adults may prefer their coffee strong or weak, but even if they don't like the taste, coffee has other uses! You can use instant, filter, or ground coffee to make ink.

COFFEE COLORS

Follow the steps below to make ink from coffee. If you leave it in the bowl for a couple of days the shade of brown will gradually darken.

1 Put the instant coffee in the small bowl.

2 Add warm water. Mix with the spoon until smooth.

3 Dip your paintbrush in the liquid and start painting on the scrap paper.

⚠ ASK AN ADULT TO ADD THE WARM WATER FOR YOU.

TIP
Use a thin brush when adding small details to your painting.

Draw a hedgehog and then use coffee ink to paint it.

See how many shades of brown you can make from your coffee ink. The longer you leave it, the darker it will get.

HEART ENVELOPES

Why not send some paintings to friends and family? Using a paper bag and your homemade coffee ink, make and decorate your very own envelopes.

1 Fold the bag in half so you get a fold line. Draw one half of a heart shape from the fold.

2 Paint a pattern over the bag. When dry, fold the bag in half and carefully cut out the shape.

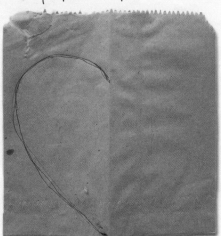

! ASK AN ADULT TO HELP WHEN USING SCISSORS.

3 You now have two hearts. Keep them together. Turn them over, patterned side down, with the point at the top. Fold the sides into the middle. Then fold the bottom up, over the middle.

Make sure the outside edges are parallel to each other.

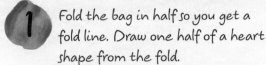

4 Separate your two envelopes. Glue the curved edges down where they overlap. Pop a painting into each envelope. Fold down the pointed flaps and seal each one with a little glue.

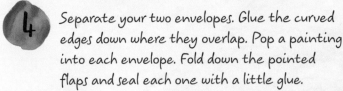

Coffee collage

A collage is made by sticking various materials together to make a new image. Make a collage using your own decorated paper.

MARK MAKING

1 Start by dipping the paintbrush in the coffee ink to make some simple dots or dashes on the paper.

2 Next, make rows of little smiles. These are perfect for illustrating bird feathers or fish scales.

3 Then, try painting some lines. Make long ones and short ones, wavy lines and loopy lines.

YOU WILL NEED

- paintbrush
- coffee ink
- brown paper

TIP
Use materials from the recycling pile, such as cardboard, scraps of paper, envelopes, and coffee filters to make your marks and lines on.

TAWNY OWL PROJECT

None of your decorated papers will go to waste! They will be used in other projects or to make the tawny owl collage below.

YOU WILL NEED
- scissors
- decorated paper
- glue

! ASK AN ADULT TO HELP WITH SCISSORS.

1 Cut out two ovals. Set one aside for the owl's body and tear the other in half to make the head. Then, cut out a triangle with a curved edge, and stick it to the head.

2 Cut out two white circles, two smaller black circles, and two even smaller white circles for the eyes. Add a triangle shape for the beak.

3 Tear two wing shapes, and add two bits of paper for the owl's feet. Now draw some claws.

4 Lastly, layer and glue all of the owl's bits and pieces together onto a piece of colored paper.

HOOT! HOOT!

tea tones

Did you know that different types of loose tea and tea bags can make a variety of sepia tones, and a whole rainbow of fruit-colored paint?

YOU WILL NEED

- 2 heaping tsp. loose tea (or a tea bag)
- 2 jars
- warm water
- coffee filter
- paintbrush
- paper

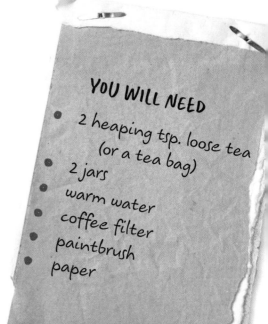

TEA COLORS

Follow the steps in this project to create your own watercolor paint. A tea bag will work just as well as loose tea. Repeat the steps with different herbal teas to make a range of colors.

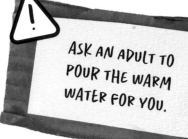

ASK AN ADULT TO POUR THE WARM WATER FOR YOU.

1 Add the loose tea into one of the jars. Add enough warm water to cover, and let soak for 10 minutes.

2 Put the filter over the other jar. Pour the tea mixture over the filter and allow the dye to drip through into the second jar.

3 Gather the edges of the filter together to squeeze the remaining liquid into the jar. Dip the brush into the liquid and start painting!

TIP
You won't need much liquid, so only slightly dampen your brush. Practice by making marks on scrap paper.

FRUITS AND FLOWERS

ASK AN ADULT WHICH PETALS AND LEAVES ARE SAFE.

HIBISCUS PETALS

MARIGOLD FLOWERS

GREEN TEA

BUTTERFLY PEA FLOWERS

Tea doesn't only come in bags, and it isn't just brown! Any dried petals and leaves that can be infused with warm water to make a flavored drink can be called tea. These loose teas make amazing paint colors.

Peppermint

Blackberry

Red bush

Purple tea

FRUITY TEA BAGS

Just look at all these impressive colors! Just soak a tea bag, fold it in half, and squeeze the color out onto your paper to make a lovely tonal wash. You can use the bag to spread the color out!

Chamomile

Strawberry

Pomegranate

Matcha

33

Fruit-tea flamingo

Now that you know that you can get colors from soggy fruit tea bags, it's time to get creative! Grab some berry tea bags to make your paint, and design your own perfectly pink flamingo.

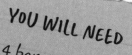

YOU WILL NEED
- 4 berry tea bags
- small bowl
- 3 tbsp. warm water
- drop of honey
- squeeze of lemon juice

⚠ ASK AN ADULT TO POUR THE WARM WATER FOR YOU.

1 Put the berry tea bags in the bowl with the warm water. Add the honey and lemon juice.

Honey

Lemon

TIP
Adding lemon juice stops the pink liquid from turning purple.

2 Wait 5–10 minutes for the liquid to turn berry colored.

3 Carefully squeeze the tea bags to release more color. You are now ready to paint.

NOW WASH YOUR PAWS!

PAINT A FLAMINGO

A flamingo is an easy bird to paint—all it takes is a splash of your pink paint and a few simple shapes.

1 Grab your paper and a paintbrush. Start by painting a rough oval shape for the flamingo's body.

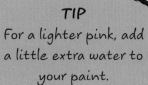

TIP
For a lighter pink, add a little extra water to your paint.

2 Now paint an "S" shape for the neck and head. Allow to dry before moving on to step 3.

3 Using a pencil, draw half a banana shape on to the head to make the beak, and fill in the end. Add a dot for the eye.

4 Paint two long, thin legs, dots for the knees, and triangular shapes for the feet. When it is all dry, finish with a pencil scribble for the wing.

Pencil scribbles add texture

Try out a stick of charcoal instead of a pencil

MORE TO MAKE

Try painting a flamingo family with fluffy, pink chicks.

Practice painting different poses

Add little details in pencil

Outline your creations

TIP
For a darker pink, add an extra layer of paint when the first coat has dried.

35

Sepia birds

You can use scrap paper patterned with tea and coffee to make a stylish little bird. We will use a traditional Indian technique to form the body shape by tying a simple overhand knot.

YOU WILL NEED

- 1 strip of patterned paper
  approx 3/4 in x 8 in (2 cm x 20 cm)
- scissors
- pencil

TIP
Try making a larger bird with a wider and longer strip.

You can create different shades of brown depending on how much tea or coffee you stain your paper with.

1 Cross the ends of the paper strip over each other. One end needs to be longer than the other.

2 Hold the paper together by pinching the place where the two pieces overlap. Pull the end of the longer piece back through the hole at the center.

3 Tug the two ends to tighten up the knot. Squash the paper down so that it's a bit flat.

4 Use scissors to shape the ends into a tail on one side and a head with a pointy beak on the other. Finish it off by adding a beady eye!

YOU CAN ADD LEGS TOO!

Nest

Also try making a nest and eggs using patterned paper and pencil marks.

MORE TO MAKE

Mushrooms

Mouse

Butterfly

Other birds

Organic inks

Just look at the fabulous colors you can extract from these delicious fruits and vegetables!

RED CABBAGE
Not just a superfood—it's also a superpowered source of artists' colors! The juice comes out purple, but can transform into green, blue, or pink with the addition of simple modifiers.

PURPLE POTATO
Guess what color we get from the unusual purple potato? Purple, of course!

ONIONS
Boiled brown onion skins make inks that range from yellow to orange, and simmered red onion skins make a range of rusty tones. Ask an adult to boil and simmer the skins.

BERRIES
Squash any berries that are too mushy to eat, and release their vibrant pink or purple pigments.

AVOCADO
Never throw away the skin of an avocado— it makes tones of pink and brown!

CARROTS
Most carrots make orange ink, but you can make yellow and purple ink from other colored carrots, too.

DRAGON FRUIT
Puree red dragon fruit to make a vibrant magenta ink.

BEET
The juice makes a rich, ruby-red ink.

LEMON
Use lemon juice as a color modifier, but also as an invisible ink. Paint secret notes with the juice, then ask an adult to iron the paper to reveal your hidden message.

KALE AND SPINACH
The high chlorophyll content in these greens makes a lush green ink.

Beeswax crayons

Did you know that you can make your very own crayons at home? These easy steps will show you how to turn beeswax into shiny, colorful crayons that will brighten up any of your pictures.

YOU WILL NEED

- ½ cup beeswax pellets or soy wax flakes
- ¼ cup pigment powder
- 1 button of cocoa butter (or ¼ tsp. coconut oil)
- empty can (washed and dried)
- saucepan
- water
- oven gloves
- popsicle stick
- mini candy mold—whatever shape you want!

TIP
Find an old food can that you can use just for making your crayons.

Beet crayon

Spirulina blue crayon

Spirulina green crayon

1 Put the beeswax, pigment, and cocoa butter into the can. Place the can into a saucepan. Pour water into the saucepan until it is about ¾ in (2 cm) up the can. Heat until the water simmers gently.

2 When all the wax and cocoa butter has melted, take the saucepan off the heat, and use oven gloves to lift the can out. Use the popsicle stick to mix everything together.

cranberry crayon

TIP
Once set, try dipping your crayon into a different colored wax mixture and see what happens.

Mold

3 Carefully, pour the mixture into your mold. Let set for 30 minutes, and then peel away the mold. Your crayon is ready!

Curcumin crayon

Color magic

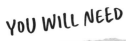
Maybe you're not a fan of cabbage, but you might change your mind when you discover all of the awesome colors that you can create from it!

EPHEMERAL INKS

Most plant-based pigments change color or fade over time. This means that they are ephemeral—they do not last very long.

When a pigment is exposed to oxygen it can change color. This is called oxidization.

Adding a natural antioxidant, such as lemon juice, to your inks makes your colors stay brighter longer.

Viridian

Teal

Magenta

Cyan

CABBAGE-COLOR CREATION

Follow the steps to create purple cabbage ink.
Then, see how you can magically modify the
ink to make a range of hues.

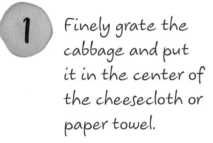

1 Finely grate the
cabbage and put
it in the center of
the cheesecloth or
paper towel.

2 Gather the edges of the cheesecloth or
paper towel and twist it into a tight
parcel. Squeeze the juice onto the plate.

3 Spoon two blobs of the ink onto a
piece of paper. Squeeze a little lemon
juice onto the first wet ink blob and
see what happens.

TIP
You could add a third
blob to see how it
changes over time.

4 Add the baking soda to the second blob and
mix it with the spoon.

Onion-skin ink

Don't throw away your papery onion skins! Whether red or brown, they can be made into a fantastic, rich ink in just a few steps.

YOU WILL NEED

- handful of onion skins
- small saucepan with lid
- water
- slotted spoon
- small strainer
- jar with lid

ASK AN ADULT TO HELP WHEN USING THE STOVE AND HOT WATER.

1 Put the skins into the saucepan with just enough water to cover them. Put the lid on and simmer over a gentle heat for 15 minutes.

2 Take the saucepan off the heat and let it sit overnight. The longer you wait, the richer the color will become.

3 Remove the skins using the slotted spoon and pop them in a compost bin if you have one. Drain the liquid through the strainer into the jar, and seal.

Red onion skin   Brown onion skin

44

MORE TO MAKE

Wild rice

Avocado skin

Beet skin

Pomegranate skin

Wild rice

Avocado skin

Beet skin

Pomegranate skin

EXPERIMENT WITH THE SKIN FROM OTHER FRUITS AND VEGETABLES. WILD RICE AND AVOCADO PITS MAKE BEAUTIFUL COLORED INKS!

Red onion skin

Spinach leaves

Avocado pits

Brown onion skin

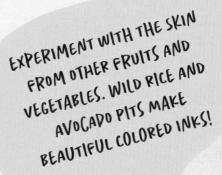

TIP
Try adding a drop of honey to make your ink smoother. Adding a dried clove or a drop of clove oil will keep your ink fresh longer.

45

Colorful creatures

Now that you have created a wonderful rainbow palette of colors, it's time to get sketching! Then, dip a paintbrush into your brightest natural inks and bring your drawings to life. Can you fill a whole page with colorful creatures?

YOU WILL NEED

- sketchbook
- pencil
- paintbrush
- black food coloring
- inks made from food
- water

paint a parrot

Black food coloring

Green cabbage

Turmeric

Beet

Turmeric and kale

Pomegranate tea

Spinach

Draw a parrot

1 Draw an arch for the head.

2 Then, draw a curved line for the body.

3 Draw a wing-shaped line, coming down from the head.

4 Add a long triangle for the tail feathers.

5 Draw the parrot's beak and claws.

6 Add the bird's eye. Then, paint your parrot!

1

Add the leeks to a saucepan, cover with water, and simmer for 30 minutes. Let them cool.

2

Meanwhile, tear the egg carton into small pieces and pop it into the blender.

Lavender

Pulp to paper

⚠️

ASK AN ADULT TO HELP WHEN USING THE STOVE, HOT WATER, AND BLENDER.

It's time to experiment with kitchen leftovers! In this simple recipe we will use egg cartons and the green parts of leeks to make our very own colored paper.

YOU WILL NEED

- 2 leek tops, roughly chopped
- saucepan
- water
- 1 empty egg carton
- blender
- large bowl
- 1 tsp. wildflower seeds
- wooden spoon
- small, flat-bottomed strainer
- paper towel

TIP
You can make different colors of paper by switching from leeks to other ingredients, such as dragon fruit or beet peels.

leek

Dragon fruit

3

Add 2 cups or water to the blender. Blend until there are no lumps. Add 3 tbsp. of leek tops in partway through.

4

Carefully pour the smooth mixture into a large bowl. Sprinkle seeds in, and give it a stir with a wooden spoon.

5

Put the strainer in the sink and pour in a layer of the pulpy mixture in one smooth action.

TIP

When you are finished with your paper, tear it up and plant it outside. In summer, the wildflower seeds should grow!

Onion skin

6

Allow the liquid to drain through the strainer, placing it on a paper towel to absorb as much moisture as possible.

Marigold and leek

7

Leave the mixture until almost dry, then carefully peel it away from the inside of the strainer. When dry, your paper is ready to use.

Beet

Leek, spinach, and kale

Creature collage

There are stacks of ideas for how to transform your homemade paper into art. Why not try cutting out various shapes, layering them, and sticking them down to create a collage?

YOU WILL NEED

- homemade paper
- scrap paper
- homemade ink
- paintbrush
- scissors
- glue
- cardboard
- pencil (optional)
- envelopes (optional)

⚠️ ASK AN ADULT FOR HELP WHEN USING SCISSORS.

BACKGROUND

The background is the part of a scene that is farthest away. Apply a wash of ink for the sky.

MIDDLE GROUND

The middle ground is the area between the background and foreground. Cut out birds from spare scraps of paper.

FOREGROUND

Items in the foreground (front) of the picture are closest to you and need to be bigger. Large cardboard leaves will complete your scene.

FRAME IT!

Stick your picture onto sturdy paper to create a fabulous frame for your art.

TIP
Arrange your shapes
into layers so you know what
needs to be glued first.

TIP
If you need more
paper, you can reuse
envelopes and cardboard.

Patterns and prints

Create wonderful patterns and prints in a few easy steps. Make some homemade ink and ask an adult to help you make simple stamps out of fruit and vegetables. Then, have fun designing your own prints!

FRUIT AND VEGETABLE PRINTING

Follow either option here, depending on what you have in the kitchen, to make a homemade ink.

FOR YOUR STAMPS

Make a fruit or vegetable stamp by carefully slicing a lemon, star fruit, okra, or potato

YOU WILL NEED—OPTION 1

- 2 tsp. natural food coloring
- 2 tsp. wheat glue or rice glue
- small bowl
- spoon
- paintbrush
- stamp made from fruit or vegetables
- paper or fabric

YOU WILL NEED—OPTION 2

- 2 tsp. spirulina powder
- 4 tsp. water
- 2 drops of honey
- small bowl
- spoon
- paintbrush
- stamp made from fruit or vegetables
- paper or fabric

Lemon

⚠️ ASK AN ADULT TO CUT UP ANY FRUIT OR VEGETABLES FOR YOU.

Star fruit

Okra

1 Put the food coloring and glue (option 1), or the spirulina powder, water, and honey (option 2), into a bowl and stir until it forms a smooth paste.

2 Use the paintbrush to apply the paste evenly onto the surface of your homemade fruit or vegetable stamp. Use it to print onto your paper or fabric.

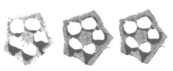

TIP
Ask an adult to cut a handle into the potato so that you can grip it easily.

potato

53

Cardboard stamps

In addition to fruit and vegetables, you can also use leftover materials, including cardboard, to make fun stamps and prints.

1 Using your pencil, draw a simple shape or character on one piece of cardboard. Carefully cut it out with scissors.

TIP
Before you glue it, decide which direction you want your printed character to face—it will print the opposite way on the page.

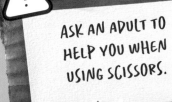

! ASK AN ADULT TO HELP YOU WHEN USING SCISSORS.

2 Glue your character onto the bigger piece of cardboard to make a stamp.

3 Using the paintbrush, cover the character with a thick layer of paint.

4 Press your stamp down onto the piece of paper to create a pattern or scene.

54

Try adding more than one color of paint to your stamp. Once your print has dried, you can also add little details.

cloud

fir tree

Rabbit

Beech tree

MORE TO MAKE

Try making up your own designs. See what other fun animals, plants, and scenes you can create!

Oak Leaf

Bee

Squirrel

Beech Leaf

55

Beach art

It's a wonderful feeling to be at the beach in all its wild weather. Whether there's bright sunshine or blustery wind, the beach is always an exciting place to explore—be it a tide-pool ramble, tideline treasure hunt, or birding with binoculars.

With sand between your toes and the sound of distant waves lapping along the shore, in this chapter we will search for charcoal, shells, and feathers to help make our art. From shiny, scaly fish prints to stunning seascapes, this habitat will spark your creativity like you wouldn't believe.

What treasures will you discover?

Charcoal

Charcoal is basically burned wood. It has been used by artists for thousands of years. This versatile material can be used for drawing, painting, and writing. Finding or making your own charcoals can be messy but fun. Eventually, you won't mind that it leaves you with dirty hands and smudges all over your art and even on the end of your nose!

Thistle

On the next page you will discover how to grind a lump of charcoal to make ink. You will then use that ink to make gorgeous landscapes and prints that experiment with light and dark tones.

A great place to find ready-made charcoal is by the cold embers of a campfire or barbecue. Come on, let's go and look...

59

Charcoal landscapes

YOU WILL NEED

- masking tape
- paper
- charcoal

Did you know that with just a little lump of charcoal you can make beautiful pictures? All you need to do is create lines, smudges, and scribbles. Let's start by drawing a seascape.

1 Tape all four edges of the paper down to create a border for your picture. Draw a horizon line, ending in a rough rectangle shape for some cliffs. A horizon line is a straight line where the land and water meet.

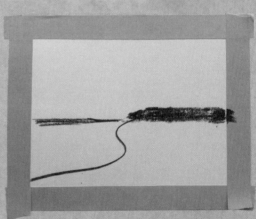

2 For the coastline, draw a long "S" shape, from the cliff to the bottom left corner of your paper. Nicely done, it's looking good!

60

3 For the sky, use the flat side of your charcoal. Move from left to right, toward the top right corner of your page—just scribble!

4 Use the side of your charcoal again, this time for the water. Then, add small dots for the sand, and some scribbly lines for grass.

5 When finished, carefully peel the tape off to reveal your spectacular seascape. You did it!

TIP
Use your fingers to smudge areas of charcoal.

Try using different sizes of charcoal sticks to create a variety of marks.

Charcoal ink

feather

Twig

Charcoal can be used in many different ways. With an adult's help, it can be ground down and transformed to create your very own ink!

Lump of charcoal

Flat stone

TIP
Make sure you don't take anything you find at the beach home with you.

1 Start by carefully grinding the charcoal on the stone to make a powder.

2 Add some water and honey for smoothness.

3 Use the remaining lump of charcoal to mix everything together.

4 Apply your ink to paper using a feather, paintbrush, or other outdoor item.

Shell

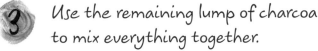

Think creatively. If you're at the beach, switch from tap water to water found at the beach, and use shells as mini paintpots!

TIP
Can't find a good paintbrush? Just use your fingertips!

fingerprints

Try using a variety of tools to see what you like best. Use a feather to paint a bird, or even seaweed to paint a picture of the shoreline!

63

Charcoal prints

Don't throw away that empty milk or juice carton! It's waterproof inside and makes an excellent printing plate that we can use with our charcoal ink.

MONOPRINT

Monoprinting is a techique that produces one singular image.

ASK AN ADULT TO HELP WHEN USING SCISSORS.

1 Use your scissors to carefully snip off the top and bottom of a clean, dry, empty carton. Cut along a side seam so that you can lay the carton flat.

2 Lay the carton on a piece of scrap paper, then brush your ink all over.

Homemade charcoal ink

TIP
Once your print is dry you can cut shapes from it. Will you make fish, butterflies, birds, or trees?

3 Lay a piece of paper on top of the inky carton and rub gently with your spoon. Peel the paper off to reveal your first monoprint.

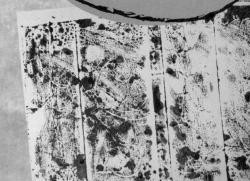

FISH PRINT

Now try cutting a simple fish shape out
of your carton before adding the ink.

1 Cut a fish shape out of the
carton to make a printing
plate. Paint the shiny side
with your ink.

2 Place your inky fish face up
and flat on a piece of scrap
paper, and lay a piece of
paper on top.

3 Use the back of the wooden
spoon to gently rub the paper
onto the printing plate in small,
circular motions.

4 Carefully peel back the
paper to reveal your
fabulously fishy print.

Rub for about
a minute.

Add a splash of color
to the background
before adding your
prints, to make your
fish stand out!

TIP
You can wipe clean
and reuse or design your fishy
printing plate to make
a whole school of fish!

Inky animals

Many animals have striking black-and-white markings. Ink is the ideal way of painting these animals, so grab your paintbrushes and let's have some fun!

Birds

Zebra

Skunk

Tapir

Penguin

Cow

Pandas

Dalmatians

Badger

PAINT A FLUFFY CHICK

A chick can have very fluffy, black-and-white feathers, making it the perfect animal to paint with splashes of ink.

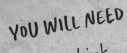

1 Using your ink, paint little dashes in a circle shape.

YOU WILL NEED

- charcoal ink
- 2 paintbrushes
- paper
- small cup of water

2 Add two dots for eyes and a small triangle beak in the center.

TIP
Add some pencil scribbles over the top for extra texture!

3 Then paint dashes in a oval-ish shape, with a slight point for the tail. Add two little "v" shapes for wings. Paint lines for the toes.

4 Using a clean, wet brush, lightly dip into your ink and make small brushstrokes to fill in the body of the bird with a feathered texture. Add more ink for darker patches. Now you have a fluffy chick!

chick

Rocks and soil

Extraordinary colors can be uncovered
from the ground beneath your feet!

In this chapter, wander through the woods or along the coast
as we head out on expeditions. Learn all about the ground
you walk on, and where to search for the best natural materials
for your art. We'll dig up a spectrum of soft, sticky clays
and a rainbow of rocks to make our own vibrant paints and
pastels. Then, together we will create some exciting pieces,
from shiny sculptures to "ancient" art.

So let's see what we can find and
make as earth explorers...

Hunting for rocks

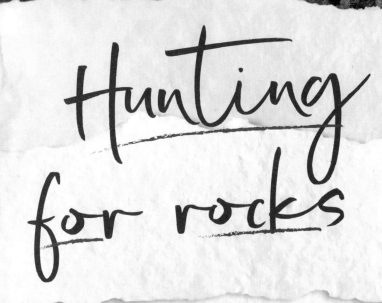

Our wonderful planet is home to soil and rocks, each with beautiful natural pigments. Colors and tones include rich reds, bright yellows, soft greens, and warm browns. But where can we find them?

HAVE AN ADULT WITH YOU WHEN YOU ARE NEAR WATER. DON'T EXPLORE UNDERNEATH ANY ROCKY CLIFFS!

ROCK HUNTING

Rocks are hidden just beneath your feet. Go to a variety of landscapes to find different rock pigments that can be used to make art.

Red sandstone

Mudstone

Red oxide

MORE TO FIND

Wander through woods to discover soil, clay, and rocks, or visit the coast to look for clay and ocher. Can you spot any of these rocks?

Mudstone

Pink slate

TIP
Go hunting for rock pigments on rainy days. Rainwater makes rock colors "pop," making them easier to find. Also, muddy pigments will turn into puddles of paint!

Red oxide

Yellow ocher

Mudstone

Green slate

Paint from green slate begins as a stone. It's crushed, and mixed with water, and a binder is added to form a paste.

Look how many different stones you can find.

See what you can draw with just a few simple stones!

ROCK COLORS

White hunting for rocks, you can also test out soil colors. They often match each other.

71

Rocks and minerals

A huge variety of richly colored rocks can be found everywhere: in the playground, in a backyard, and by the coast. Some rocks have a bright pigment to share, while others are great for making scratchy marks.

Some rocks are soft and chalky—perfect for using like a pastel.

TIP
Use a hard rock as a surface to test out your colors.

Red ocher

Some are medium-hard and make scratchy marks.

Pencil slate

Others need to be rubbed with water to release color.

Red oxide

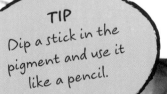

A few are so hard that you would need a hammer to crush the pigment out!

Black slate

TIP
Dip a stick in the pigment and use it like a pencil.

WHY NOT TRY

- Pebble sculpture art
- Paint a picture of your surroundings
- Log your findings in your sketchbook

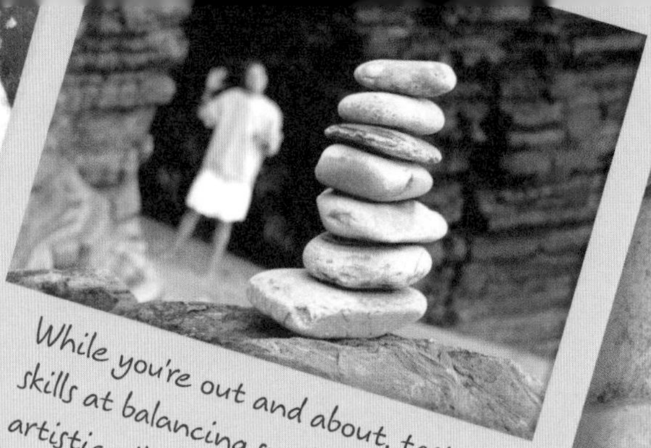

While you're out and about, test your skills at balancing small stones in artistic piles, like this one.

Go on a rock treasure hunt and find amazing colors from yellows to greens and browns to grays!

Yellow sandstone

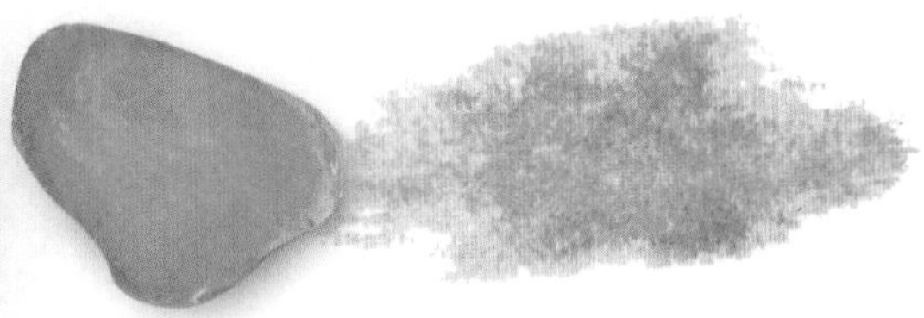

Green slate

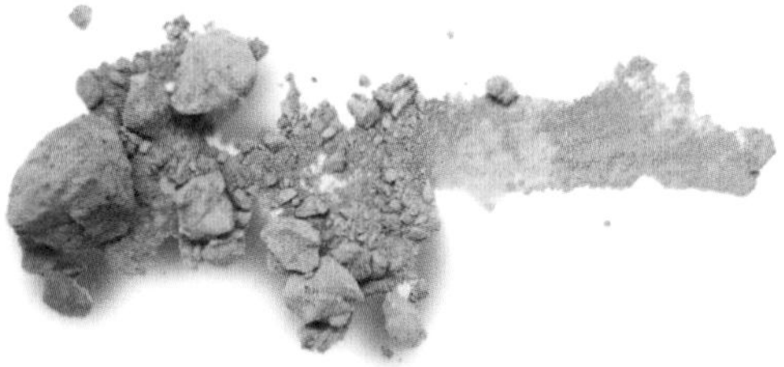

Mudstone

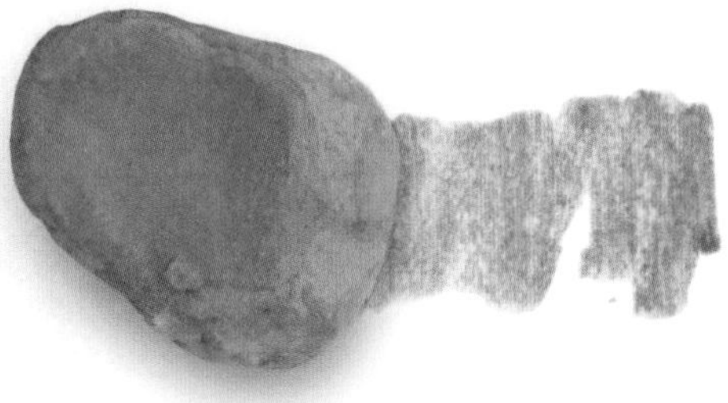

Graphite

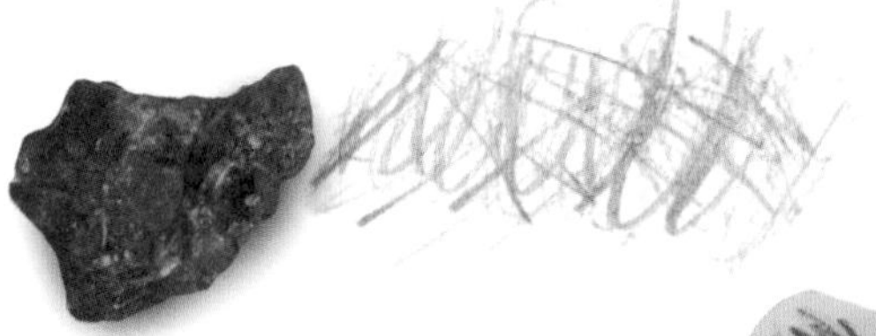

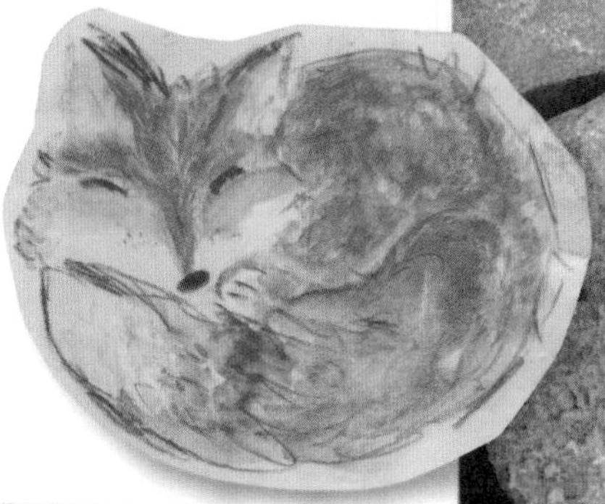

MORE TO MAKE

Using the pigments from rocks, you can also color paper and paint your favorite animals.

ALWAYS HAVE AN ADULT WITH YOU WHEN NEAR WATER. ONLY TAKE WHAT YOU NEED FROM NATURE. ASK AN ADULT TO USE THE HAMMER, AND WEAR SAFETY GOGGLES TO PROTECT YOUR EYES. THEY CAN WRAP THE ROCKS IN PAPER AND PLACE THEM IN AN OLD SOCK, BEFORE POUNDING WITH THE HAMMER.

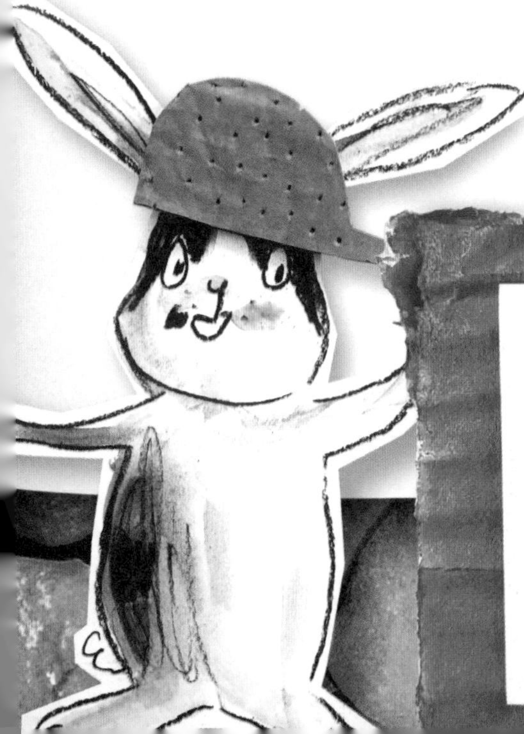

Rock paints

Hunting for interesting rocks and testing which ones have a color is so exciting! Soft, colored rocks can make a range of natural paint colors that can be used to make art—here's how!

YOU WILL NEED
- soft, colored rocks
- water
- paintbrush
- paper

1 Find and collect a few soft, colored rocks.

chalk is a soft rock

2 Dip each rock into some water. This will make your paint.

3 Using your paintbrush, rub the water into each rock. Now, you have colored rock paints and can paint a picture!

TIP
To test if a stone has a color, rub it against another stone.

Red ocher

MORE TO MAKE
Search for different colored rocks and try crushing the rocks between two stones to make a pigment powder. You can add a little water to this powder to make colorful paints.

ASK AN ADULT TO HELP WHEN CRUSHING ROCKS.

Pastel chalk

Pastel chalk is great for drawing with because it is easy to blend and can also add detail to a picture. It can be used wet or dry and comes in many colors. Use these steps to make your very own pastel chalk.

YOU WILL NEED

- small bowl
- handful of clay found in soil or kaolin clay
- 1 tsp. gum arabic medium
- 1 tbsp. water
- wooden spoon

1 Put your clay into a bowl.

2 Add the gum arabic medium and water to the clay. Mix it together using a spoon.

⚠️ MAKE SURE TO TEST THE SOIL BEFOREHAND IF YOU LIVE IN AN AREA WHERE THERE IS A RISK OF CONTAMINATION.

MORE TO MAKE

There are many different colors of chalk that you can make depending on the clay you use. You can also add pigments for color.

This pastel chalk is made from green clay. Matcha powder was added to make this green chalk brighter.

These pastels are made using different colors of soil.

TIP
If you have some mixture left over, just add a drop of water and use it like a watercolor paint.

3 Keep stirring until the mixture binds together enough for you to pick up in your hands.

4 Roll it between your palms to form a ball shape and leave your pastel chalk on the windowsill for a few days to dry. Now it's time to draw!

Animal prints

Cut an animal shape from a piece of cardboard, put it against your paper, and cover it with your rock paints. When you remove the cardboard, you'll have a space to fill with fun little details. You can also keep the outer stencil, so that nothing is wasted!

YOU WILL NEED

- pencil
- cardboard
- scissors
- water
- sponge or paintbrush
- soft, colored rock
- paper

⚠ ASK AN ADULT TO HELP YOU CUT OUT YOUR ANIMAL SHAPE.

1 Using a pencil, draw a duckling shape on your cardboard, with a circle for the head and a triangle for the beak.

2 Next, cut your shape out carefully, so you have a cardboard duckling.

3 Wet your sponge or paintbrush and rub over the rock to make paint.

MORE TO MAKE

Bear

Elephant

Giraffe

Cat

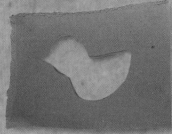

Outer stencil

TIP
Try using the outer stencil to make more art! How is it different from the prints on this page?

4 Now, place the duckling on top of a piece of paper. Using your wet sponge, paint all over it.

5 Finished? Now carefully lift up the duckling shape.

6 Scribble in some texture and details and you have made your duckling art!

Cave art

Cave paintings are the earliest record of art in history. They were made using colors (pigments) from rocks, stones, and burned wood. Make your own "ancient" art with a couple of tea bags and some colorful rocks.

⚠ ASK AN ADULT TO HELP WHEN USING WARM WATER AND BREAKING ROCKS.

1 Put the tea bags in a jar and add a little warm water. Leave them for 10 minutes.

2 Just look at the rich color! Rub the tea bags all over the paper to stain it. Let it dry.

3 Now make some paint! Break your colorful rocks into small pieces using a mortar and pestle.

4 Mix together the small, soft pieces of rock and 2 tbsp. warm water. Now you have your paint.

NOW USE YOUR PAINT TO MAKE CAVE CHARACTERS ON YOUR TEA-STAINED PAPER.

TIP
Keep some dry charcoal handy and add simple characters and details to your art.

TIP
Ochers are soft and chalky, and can be used like pastels on your tea-stained paper.

Sanguine ocher

Yellow ocher

Dampen larger rocks and scribble directly onto your paper.

Red ocher

Try applying paint with sticks.

Furry friends

What creatures might you find hiding in the woods? Create adorable art showcasing your furry friends. Make simple pencil or charcoal sketches, then bring your drawings to life, using paints made from rocks and soil.

charcoal stick

1 First, draw an oval-ish shape for the body.

2 Next, draw two little ears, and a dash for the nose.

3 Draw in some little lines for the paws, and a dot for the eye.

4 Add some whiskers and a long tail. Now you're ready to paint.

Red ocher

Green slate pastel

Red oxide rock

MORE TO MAKE
Try sketching more furry friends, using these pictures as a guide. Paint your drawings and allow to dry before adding extra details in pencil or charcoal.

Bat

Doe

Rabbit

Fox

Squirrel

Shrew

Mouse

5 Paint your mouse using different shades of natural paint to add texture. Now your picture is complete!

Dorodango

Mud can be used in many different ways. In Japan, artists mix mud and water together to make shiny ball sculptures. This art is called "dorodango."

⚠ ASK AN ADULT BEFORE DIGGING IN THE YARD.

TIP
To make your sculptures colorful, try adding a pigment. Turmeric or spirulina powder work well.

YOU WILL NEED

- handful of wet clayish mud or clay soil
- few pieces of dry grass
- few drops of water
- bowl
- handful of loose, dry mud
- small jar

1 Dig up wet mud from the yard. Make sure to pick out any debris like stones or roots.

2 Add dry grass to the mud. Squash the mixture, then roll it between your hands.

3 Keep rolling the mixture until it looks like a ball. Let it dry in the sun or on a windowsill for about three hours, or until it's dry to touch.

TIP
Your ball should be big enough to rest on the opening of your jar.

4 Put water on your hands and roll the mud ball between your palms. Put loose, dry mud in a bowl and roll the ball around until it's covered in mud.

5 Place the ball on the rim of an open jar and carefully roll it in a circular motion. The rim compresses and polishes the mud to make it smoother and shinier.

6 Repeat steps 4 and 5 a few more times. When your ball is super shiny, you're finished!

TIP
Rub your ball with a cloth to add even more shine!

Plant colors

I love flowers! From delicate, purple sweet peas and elegant, pink lilies to bold and bright yellow sunflowers, they are so varied, beautiful, and brilliant. Don't you just wish flowers could last forever?

In this chapter, we'll harvest those lovely pigments—pressing and mashing sunshine hues out of gorgeous flowers to make art. We'll learn how to use the colors from petals and leaves to dye our own fabrics, and we'll find fresh flowers to create botanical prints and patterns with.

It feels wonderful to take flowers and leaves that are already fabulous in their natural form and use them to make art. So, what are you waiting for? Let's get started...

ALWAYS CHECK WHICH FLOWERS AND LEAVES ARE OKAY TO PICK.

Solar dyeing

Solar dyeing is a natural way to dye fabric or yarn using flower petals, leaves, and heat from the sun!

YOU WILL NEED

- handful of dried petals and leaves
- clean, empty jar
- 1 tsp. salt
- small piece of plain white fabric or yarn
- cold water

Dried hibiscus petals

1 First, collect fallen petals and leaves.

2 Put these petals and leaves in your jar and add salt.

3 Add the fabric and cold water, so that the jar is about half full.

4 Put the jar out in the sun or on a windowsill, and wait a few days. Squeeze out the water, then dry the fabric out to see the results.

Using dandelion flowers in your dye will turn it bright yellow. You can then use the leftover water to paint vibrant yellow characters.

Dandelion

Scrap paper

Dyed cloth

Black bean

You can also use some foods to dye your fabric and yarn. Despite their name, when used as a dye black beans make a deep-purple color.

Dyed yarn

MORE TO MAKE

Experiment with different petals, leaves, and even peels, and see what colors of fabric or yarn you can make.

Onion skins

Beet peels

Rose petals

Black beans

Cosmos petals

Meadowsweet petals

Marigold petals

Dragon fruit skin

89

Flower power

Botanical colors can be taken from fallen petals, herb garden leaves, and more. For a quick burst of color, just rub petals and leaves directly onto your crafts or, if you have time, make your own flower-powered ink and paint.

YOU WILL NEED

- petals and leaves
- plain, fabric bag

FLOWER INK

An easy way to use botanical colors is to rub them directly onto fabric.

1 Gather a selection of colorful petals and fallen leaves.

2 Rub each one onto your fabric bag and watch the vibrant colors transfer.

Mint leaf

TIP
You can use botanical ink to transform an old white t-shirt, too.

fabric bags

Roses

WATERCOLOR PAINT

You've already learned how to use your petals to make solar-dyed ink (see p.88–89). Now, let's turn your ink into watercolor paint.

(see p.88–89)

YOU WILL NEED

- coffee filter
- jar
- 3 tbsp. homemade solar-dyed ink (see p.88–89)
- 1 tsp. watercolor medium that's ready to use (gum arabic or gum tragacanth)

(see p.88–89)

1 Put a piece of the coffee filter over the top of the jar.

2 Next, carefully add your solar-dyed ink to the jar.

3 Stir in the watercolor medium and your paint is ready to use!

TIP
Add some clove oil to your ink to make it last longer.

TIP
When you add your watercolor medium, your ink becomes paint!

Watercolor paint

Inks

Rose hips

Marigolds

Dahlias

Flower pounding

Flower pounding, also called "tataki-zomé," is the Japanese art of hammering flowers to create patterns on fabric. Let's try it! Ask an adult where you can pick a few colorful flowers, then create your very own printed pattern.

> ⚠️ **ASK AN ADULT TO HELP WHEN HAMMERING.**
> BE SURE TO CHECK WITH AN ADULT WHICH PLANTS AND LEAVES ARE SAFE TO USE IN YOUR ART.

1 Lay your fabric on top of a piece of cardboard. Next, position a flower on the fabric, making sure it's face down.

YOU WILL NEED

- plain fabric
- cardboard
- fresh flowers or leaves
- parchment paper (or paper towel)
- small hammer

2 Cover your flower with parchment paper or paper towel.

3 Gently hammer the flower until it is flat and the shape and color have transferred onto the fabric.

4 Carefully peel off the parchment paper and flower to reveal your printed fabric. Do the same with more flowers to create a pretty pattern.

TIP
This technique works on paper too.

Pressed flowers

If you don't have a fancy flower press, don't let that stop you—a heavy book works just as well! Then, fill your journal with pressed leaves and flowers that remind you of the beautiful places you've visited.

Blotting paper

TIP
Avoid chunky flowers or succulent leaves because they hold a lot of water and can get moldy!

Cosmos

forget-me-not

YOU WILL NEED

- blotting paper
- blank book
- flowers and leaves
- heavy book

Pansy

Mint

Lavender

TIP
Don't overlook smaller flowers, grasses, and even weeds—they often have beautiful shapes.

⚠ ASK AN ADULT WHICH FLOWERS ARE OKAY TO PICK.

1 Place a sheet of blotting paper on an open page of your blank book. Arrange a few flowers and leaves on the paper.

2 Cover the flowers with another sheet of blotting paper, then carefully close the book. Put a heavy book on top to weigh it down.

3 Leave the flowers and leaves for a week, or until they are flat, dry, and beautiful!

WHY NOT TRY
- Make a greeting card
- Create a gift tag
- Make framed art

95

Flower painting

Painting flowers and other natural objects can be great fun! You can make beautiful art by using the homemade paints and inks that you extracted from flower petals and leaves.

There is a variety of leaf shapes to discover and paint.

Get inspiration from the different colors and tones that can be found in leaves—from vibrant lime to nearly black!

Find flowers with interesting colors and shapes, and practice painting them.

1 With a paintbrush or a twig, first practice painting circles, stars, and straight lines.

2 Start your flower by painting a neat circle with purple paint.

3 Then, use a twig to scratch small star shapes into the paint.

4 Finally, paint a long green line for the flower stem. Good job!

MORE TO MAKE

Fruit and vegetables are fun to paint, too! Practice drawing and painting radishes, cabbages, apples, and more.

Radishes

Cabbage

BUNNIES LOVE TO EAT RADISHES.

Apple

Did you know?
Some flowers, including tulips and crocuses, close their petals at night to keep their pollen safe and dry.

Petal patterns

Everywhere we look in nature we can find amazing patterns and designs. Why not gather a few flowers and petals and make a pattern of your own! Here's how you get started...

1 Find a flower and place it face up in the center of a piece of paper or just on a flat, clean surface.

North

West   East

South

2 Find four matching petals and place them north, east, south, and west around the flower.

3 Now select eight smaller petals. Place them on both sides of each of the four petals you've already put down.

WELL DONE. YOU'VE STARTED YOUR FIRST PATTERN!

KEEP ADDING PETALS TO MAKE A FUN PATTERN LIKE THE ONES SHOWN ABOVE.

TIP
When you're finished, reuse your petals and leaves to create a completely different design.

Fall crafts

Looking for some fun fall activities? Follow in the footsteps of famous artist Leonardo da Vinci and make your own oak-gall or walnut ink. Or, create a homemade loom and learn how to weave.

AUTUMNAL INK

Oak galls can only be found on oak trees, and are made by the larvae of oak-gall wasps.

YOU WILL NEED

- oak galls, or walnut husks
- old sock
- rolling pin
- saucepan
- water
- strainer
- 1 tbsp gum arabic
- filter paper
- jar

TIP
Leave a container outside to collect rainwater, then use it in this activity.

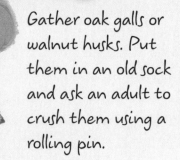

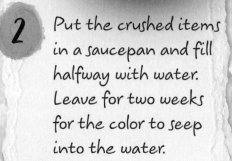

1 Gather oak galls or walnut husks. Put them in an old sock and ask an adult to crush them using a rolling pin.

2 Put the crushed items in a saucepan and fill halfway with water. Leave for two weeks for the color to seep into the water.

3 Strain out the bits, and stir in the gum arabic. Pour the liquid through filter paper into a jar. Use the ink to paint or write with.

LOOM

Fall is a great time for collecting fallen twigs. Use yours to make a loom and learn the art of weaving.

1 Gather four straight twigs of equal size.

2 Arrange the twigs in a square shape. Tie each corner together with string so the loom holds its shape.

3 Wrap more string around the frame, weaving from one side to the other. Tie and cut the string at the bottom left corner.

4 Arrange your flowers, leaves, and other found objects, weaving them into the string. Hang up your loom for some fall decoration!

Bundle dyeing

Did you know you can create patterned fabric from flowers, leaves, and petals? Follow these steps to add a splash of natural color to your fabric.

YOU WILL NEED

- 2 cups (500 ml) water, plus extra for steaming
- 2 tbsp. salt
- bowl
- plain, white piece of cotton fabric
- flowers, leaves, and petals
- parchment paper
- rolling pin
- string
- food steamer with lid

1 Pour the water and salt into a bowl. Submerge your fabric and soak it for 30 minutes.

2 Take the fabric out, and squeeze the water out. Arrange your flowers, leaves, and petals on top of the fabric.

3 Lay a piece of parchment paper on top of the flowers, then roll the rolling pin over the paper to flatten everything.

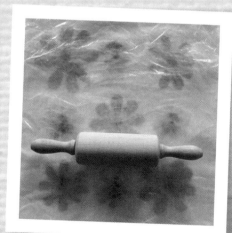

4 Roll the layers up into a sausage shape and wind the string around to hold it all together. Curl your fabric into a bundle and secure with more string.

5 Pour cold water into the bottom of the steamer and put it on the stove. Put the bundle in the tray and steam for 30 minutes. Turn off the heat and leave the bundle in the steamer for an hour or two to let it cool.

ASK AN ADULT TO STEAM THE BUNDLE. DON'T REUSE THE STEAMER FOR COOKING FOOD AFTER USING IT TO MAKE ART.

flower-dyed fabric

6 Remove the bundle from the steamer, take off the string, roll out your fabric, and remove the flowers and parchment paper. Let your fabric dry in the sun. Wow, look at your colorful fabric!

Botanical monoprints

This project is a great way to use petals and leaves that you've found to make beautiful botanical art. We will be monoprinting, which means every single print will be different!

TIP
To flatten your leaves or petals, put paper towels on both sides of them and pop them inside a heavy book for an hour or two.

1 Place a leaf on a piece of cardboard. Take your paintbrush and paint one side of the leaf in whatever color you want.

Test print with both sides of the leaf to see which looks best.

Sage Leaf

2 Carefully pick up your leaf, and place it face up on a piece of scrap paper. Lay your monoprinting paper on top.

Scrap paper

Monoprinting paper

Oxalis petal

3 Use the back of a spoon to rub the monoprinting paper in a circular motion, pressing evenly. The longer you do this, the better your print will be!

Acer

4 Gently peel back the monoprinting paper and let it dry. Look, you have made a monoprint!

Print small leaves and petals to create insect wings.

Strawberry leaf

You can use the same piece of paper for many monoprints to create colorful patterns or scenes.

Go explore

Look out of the window—it's a beautiful day!
Should we head out on a journey to explore
our wonderful natural world?

Whether you find yourself by the ocean, in the woods,
or in a backyard, nature generously provides us with
inspiration. Nature also gifts us an abundance of art
materials that we can use: twig drawing sticks,
seashell paintpots, and muddy mixtures.

Come on, let's see what we can find...

Explorers' tools

Before heading outside, you'll need to gather some tools from home. So, grab your coat, pack a bag, and go exploring with an adult.

SUNSCREEN

If the weather forecast is for sunshine then remember to apply sunscreen. Reapply when you're out and about.

OUTDOOR CLOTHES

Wrap up warm if it's cold, and wear something waterproof if it's raining. Wear walking shoes or boots to keep your feet comfortable and dry, and a pair of gloves when collecting things.

BACKPACK OR SATCHEL

Find a comfortable but sturdy bag. It should be waterproof and big enough to carry everything you might possibly need or find. Who knows what you might come across?

SKETCHBOOK

You never know when inspiration might strike! Keep your sketchbook and pencils handy, to draw any landscapes, animals, or plants that catch your eye.

BINOCULARS

Binoculars are great for observing animals from a distance, so you don't startle them. Try bird-watching. What birds can you see in the trees?

SNACKS AND WATER

Always carry a bottle of water, especially in hot weather. Pack a few snacks so that you don't get hungry if you're exploring for long periods of time.

PAPER BAGS FOR FORAGING

You can collect rocks, sticks, and flowers and store them until you are ready to make your art.

JOURNAL AND TAPE

Make a collage to show off what you find when exploring! Use clear tape to stick foraged items, such as leaves and flowers, into your journal.

REMEMBER TO BE CAREFUL ABOUT WHAT YOU TOUCH, AND ALWAYS FORAGE WITH AN ADULT.

MAGNIFYING GLASS

Get up close to any insects you might discover by using your magnifying glass. See how many little details you can spot, and then sketch!

In the backyard

Do you have a backyard, a window box, or a park nearby? These are all great places to get closer to nature and observe wildlife, big and small.

FLOWERS
Sprinkle wildflower seeds into a pot, window box, or flower bed. Pollinators, such as bees, will love to visit and slurp on the delicious, sweet nectar!

GRASS
Feel the texture of grass under your bare feet. Is it soft, wet, or tickly?

BUGS
Use a magnifying glass to examine ants, beetles, or caterpillars. Count the spots on a ladybug's back, or admire the spirals on a snail's shell.

NIGHT SKY

At sunrise or sunset, watch the sky change color. Look for patterns, called constellations, in the twinkly stars.

CLOUDS

Look up at the sky. In the daytime you might see clouds floating past. Do any look like funny animal shapes?

YOU WILL NEED

- large handful of wildflower seeds
- bowl
- few handfuls of mud
- water

MAKE A SEED BOMB

By following these simple steps, you can make seed bombs to scatter in your yard, and grow wildflowers.

ANIMALS

Find inspiration for your sketchbook by studying a dog, cat, chicken, rabbit, hedgehog, or even a teeny, tiny mouse.

1 Put the seeds into the bowl with the mud.

2 Mix everything together. Add water until the mixture starts to stick together.

3 Roll the mixture into balls. Allow to dry overnight.

BIRDS

Build a shelter, called a bird blind, so that you can sneakily watch birds. Scatter a few oats or raisins to attract more visitors. How many different varieties can you spot?

4 Scatter the balls on soil (where allowed), and wait for your flowers to grow.

Bug hotel

Creepy-crawlies, such as bees and butterflies, are beautiful and also essential to life as we know it. But they need our help! Many species of bugs are in decline because their habitats have been destroyed, so let's build them a safe place to live.

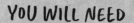

YOU WILL NEED

- old plant pot
- cardboard
- dry, hollow plant stems
- wood with holes in it
- straw
- dry leaves
- twigs
- moss

ASK AN ADULT TO MAKE A HOLE IN YOUR PLANT POT. !

TIP
You can use a wooden crate instead of a plant pot.

1. Find an old terra-cotta pot. Make a hole in the bottom of the pot if it doesn't have one already.

2 Pack your pot with items from the list, including cardboard, hollow plant stems, wood with holes in it, straw, dry leaves, twigs, and moss.

Straw for ladybugs

Hollow stems and wood for bees

Rolled cardboard with room for bigger bugs

I'LL JUST BE STAYING ONE NIGHT, THANKS!

Dry Leaves and twigs for beetles

Moss to fill spaces

TIP
Add a variety of materials to your hotel to attract lots of different bugs.

3 Lay the pot on its side in a sheltered spot at the far end of your backyard. Wait for passing bugs to crawl inside and rest in their new home.

113

At the beach

On a trip to the beach there is endless inspiration, plus lots of natural art materials to discover. Search for shells to use as paintpots, and burned driftwood for charcoal. Remember to leave everything you find on the beach for others to enjoy.

CLAY

At low tide, the waves often expose deposits of soft clay near the waterline. Form a ball of clay into a little cup, scoop up some water, and mix it with your brush to make an instant watercolor paint!

CHARCOAL

Lumps of burned driftwood are often washed up by the tide or left over from a campfire. You can use them to sketch a scene.

By applying different levels of pressure you can make darker or lighter lines.

NEVER EXPLORE RIGHT UNDER A CLIFF WHERE LOOSE ROCKS MAY FALL! THE BEACH CAN BE DANGEROUS TOO—ALWAYS EXPLORE WITH AN ADULT.

PEBBLES

Look for soft stones or pebbles, worn smooth by the ocean. Test them to see if they are good for mark-making by rubbing them on a hard, flat rock.

SEAWEED

Washed up pieces of seaweed and sponges can make wonderful paintbrushes! Just tie some onto a stick of driftwood and see what marks you can make.

Find a handful of seaweed on a beach, and some fishing rope or twine and make your own paintbrushes.

PAINTPOTS

Shells are the perfect shape to use as containers for the paint you make at the beach.

Look at the colors and tones of the shells, and recreate the same shades in your art.

SHELLS

Nature has decorated these shells with lines and dots and spirals. Can you copy some of these shapes in your art?

WHY NOT TRY

- Use a stick to draw patterns in the wet sand
- Make little characters out of any sea debris you find

Driftwood

Beach canvases

Left your sketchbook at home? See what natural canvases you can find to paint on at the beach. Grab your paintbrush and your soft, colored rocks, and get painting.

YOU WILL NEED

- leaves
- driftwood
- stones
- soft, colored rocks
- water from the beach
- flat stone
- paintbrush

BE WITH AN ADULT AT THE BEACH. DON'T GO UNDER CLIFFS. IT IS ILLEGAL TO TAKE MANY NATURAL MATERIALS FROM A BEACH, SO DO ACTIVITIES THERE.

1 Gather some leaves, driftwood, and stones to paint on.

TIP
Use driftwood and stones with a flat edge, to make painting easier.

2 Dip your soft rocks into water and rub them against a flat stone to make a chalky paint.

3 Dip your paintbrush in, and paint patterns such as lines, dots, or dashes, on your unique natural canvases.

In the woods

Nature is an artist's pantry, packed full of painter's pigments and drawing tools. Let's wander through the woods and discover fascinating textures, sights, sounds, and smells.

TREES

There are so many varieties, from evergreen conifers with pointy needles, to broad-leaved deciduous trees. Take note of the shapes and sizes of trees you see.

LEAVES

Leaves come in thousands of different tones and shades that change with the seasons. Store fallen leaves in your journal and use them in your future art projects.

TWIGS

Fallen twigs can be used as drawing sticks, paintbrush handles, looms, or frames for your art.

BARK

Feel the texture with your fingertips. Is the bark rough and bumpy, or shiny and smooth? Hold a sheet of paper against the trunk and rub it with charcoal to capture the tree's unique "fingerprint."

CHARCOAL

Some artists make charcoal from the logs and twigs in their own yard. Charcoal varies in hardness depending on the type of wood it's made from.

MUD

Mud colors vary from place to place. Mix a little mud with a splash of water, and remember to paint a color swatch in your journal wherever you go.

ANIMALS

Can you hear rustling in the undergrowth? Are there tiny paw prints in the mud? If you stay quiet and don't move, you might see deer, rabbits, squirrels, or foxes to sketch!

LICHENS

These organisms have traditionally been used to dye fabrics, such as tweed. How many different types can you find and sketch in your journal?

BIRDS

You will hear and see different birds at different times of the day or year. Listen for hooting owls and trilling songbirds. Go bird-watching and record what you see.

119

Den building

Would you like to make your own hideout? You could use it as a bird blind and go bird-watching, or as a secret den to watch woodland creatures. If you're quiet and patient, who knows what you may see?

YOU WILL NEED

- long branches
- sturdy tree
- rope

⚠ ALWAYS HAVE AN ADULT WITH YOU WHEN EXPLORING THE WOODS. ASK AN ADULT TO HELP YOU HANDLE HEAVY BRANCHES AND SECURE THEM SAFELY AGAINST THE TREE.

1 Look around and collect some long, straight branches from the forest floor.

2 Choose a strong tree with forked branches that you can easily prop branches up against.

3 Make a frame by propping three similar-sized branches against the tree. Ask an adult to make sure that they're stable. You can use rope to secure the branches in place.

4 Place more branches alongside the first ones, leaving a space for the entrance.

5 Keep adding branches and filling spaces in your structure until it starts to look like a tepee. Ask an adult to secure the branches.

6 Good job, your den is ready!

TIP
When finished, add little twigs with leaves to camouflage your den and make it cosy.

YOU ARE A NATURAL ARTIST!

I'm sure that you've discovered new ways of seeing the natural wonders all around you. Maybe you've tried using a twig pencil or seaweed paintbrush, made paint from rocks or petals, or experimented with some other new techniques. Wherever you go, and whatever you create, remember to have fun, be safe, and take care of our precious planet.

You are the future, and you can be a caretaker of our environment by observing nature closely. Celebrate its wondrous designs, forms, patterns, and colors in your art, and use its resources responsibly. Remember to reuse and recycle whenever possible. Leave the places you explore just as you found them, ready for the next adventurer to enjoy.

So, my fellow natural artist, the time has come for you to GO EXPLORE, HAVE FUN, and don't forget to take your journal everywhere you go and fill it with wonderful stuff!

Pippa xx

GLOSSARY

artwork
any piece of art, such as a painting, collage, or sculpture

binder
substance that helps materials stick together

blending
mixing two or more substances together to become one

botanical
substance from or relating to plants and flowers

chalk
type of soft white rock that can be used as a drawing tool. Other materials can also have a chalky consistency.

charcoal
charred twigs or sticks, that are black and used as a drawing tool

charring
to burn or scorch a surface. Part of the process that turns wood into charcoal

composition
arrangement of items in a picture. For example, how animals, trees, and other shapes are arranged in a piece of art

contrast
when two or more things have clear differences when compared

cool colors
colors with a cold, bluish tone

crosshatching
crisscrossing lines to mark or shade objects or scenes

depth (color)
the strength and intensity of a color

design
arranged pattern. Also a plan for how something might look when it is finished

detail
just one small part of a picture or work, not the whole thing

extract
to remove something from something else. For example, citric acid from lemon juice

horizon
line where the ocean or land appear to meet the sky

hue
another word for color

ink
liquid used for writing or painting, it can be black or colored

landscape (format)
when rectangular paper is wider than it is tall

layering
placing one or more items on top of each other, such as paper in a collage or coats of paint

medium
material that is used by an artist, for example pencil, ink, or paint

mineral
naturally occurring substance. Rocks from the ground generally contain two or more minerals, which can be used as pigments

modifier
in art, a substance used to change the state of another

monoprint
a printing technique where only one final image is made

oil paint
paint made by mixing pigment and oil. It dries slowly, so it is easy to make changes and fix mistakes

oxidized
when a substance changes
because of coming into contact
with oxygen. The process is
called oxidization

palette
any surface or container that
is suitable for mixing paint. Also
used to describe the range of
colors used by a painter

pastel
drawing stick made from
pigments that have been
bound together with gum.
Soft pastels are powdery and
often called chalk pastels

pattern
decorative design in which the
same shape or sequence of
shapes are regularly repeated
on a surface

pigment
substance used to give
something a particular color

portrait (format)
when rectangular paper is
taller than it is wide

print
art made by pressing an
object onto a surface and
leaving a mark

pulp
objects that have been crushed
into a paste

recycle
taking something used and
turning it into something else,
rather than throwing it away

reuse
to use something more than once

rough paper
paper with a textured surface

scrap paper
leftover paper

seascape
painting, picture, or sketch
with a view of the sea

sepia
deep, reddish-brown pigment
or color

shade
darkness of a color. Dark
sections in a picture may also
be called shading

smooth paper
paper with a flat, even surface

texture
feel of a surface, or when things
in a picture look like they would
feel a certain way, such as rough
or smooth

tint
lightness of a color, made
by adding white

tone
range of lighter or darker
shades of a color

tragacanth
natural gummy material that
comes from a spiny shrub and
binds substances together

warm colors
colors with a red or
orange tone

wash
layer of one flat color across
the page, used especially
in watercolor

watercolor
thin paint made by mixing
pigment and water, often used
for light, see-through effects

INDEX

Acknowledgments

DK would like to thank Catherine Saunders for
proofreading, Anne Damerell for legal guidance,
and Helen Peters for compiling the index. DK would also like
to thank Joel Pixley, Matt Denham, Nellie Shepherd for
additional photography and Eden Pixley for art assistance.
A special mention goes out to Bullclough Art School,
The Dove Valley Centre, and Denham Peaks Ltd
(Home Farm, Hollinsclough) for sharing their location
spaces with the author.

Pippa would like to thank the super team at DK, her lovely
friends and family for all their support, and her wonderful,
inspirational pets!

The publisher would like to thank the following for their kind permission to reproduce their photographs:
(Key: a-above; b-below/bottom; c-center; f-far; l-left; r-right; t-top)

12-13 Dreamstime.com: Roberaten / Roberto Atencia Gutierrez. **15 Dreamstime.com:** Nevinates (cb). **Getty Images:** (tl).
21 Dreamstime.com: Robynmac / Robyn Mackenzie (b). **46 Dreamstime.com:** Robynmac / Robyn Mackenzie (t). **56-59
Dreamstime.com:** Viacheslav Voloshyn. **Getty Images / iStock:** Paperkites (white paper). **66-69 Getty Images / iStock:** Paperkites.
68 Dreamstime.com: Roberaten / Roberto Atencia Gutierrez (b). **72 Getty Images / iStock:** Paperkites (t). **76-77 Dreamstime.com:**
Roberaten / Roberto Atencia Gutierrez (Paper). **Getty Images / iStock:** Paperkites. **80 Getty Images / iStock:** Paperkites (t).
82 Getty Images / iStock: Paperkites (t). **84 Getty Images / iStock:** Paperkites (t). **86-87 123RF.com:** stillfx. **86 Dreamstime.com:**
Robynmac / Robyn Mackenzie (tl). **94-95 Dreamstime.com:** Drsupaksorn / Suphaksorn Thongwongboot (t). **94 123RF.com:** stillfx.
97 Getty Images / iStock: Paperkites. **100 Getty Images / iStock:** Paperkites. **106 Getty Images / iStock:** Paperkites. **107 Dorling
Kindersley:** Stephen Oliver (br). **110-111 Getty Images / iStock:** Paperkites. **111 Dorling Kindersley:** Robin Chittenden (clb). **114-115
Getty Images / iStock:** Paperkites. **118-119 Getty Images / iStock:** Paperkites. **119 Dreamstime.com:** Roman Ivaschenko (clb)

All other images © Dorling Kindersley